THIS IS NOT TOPSOIL

SARA BISSEN

ARTENA ANARCHIST PRESS

This Is Not Topsoil

ISBN 9788894050561

CONTENTS

We See Only
What Has Been Produced for Us to See

Kelly Nosari

Tacit acceptance of the commodities and information that inundate our urban lives promises control over the chaos. In reality, it prevents us from seeing beyond the surface of things to understand our complicity in the world we inhabit. In this hall of mirrors, we are removed from the reality that we are all actors, whatever role we play in the hierarchy of exchange. Sara Bissen's *Topsoil* deliberately challenges such inertia by revealing the global commodity chain of capital that underpins our lives.

Topsoil is at once essay, book, critique, and artist manifesto. It is also none of these things. It is most certainly a dense read—in content and in structure. Introduced as a play, sources are given as a list of characters, names scrambled and removed from their context. It follows the story of cotton from the farmer planting the seed in the soil in India to the all-powerful urban marketplace in New York City—revealing the urban dweller's separation from actual global systems. At the same time, the text is not linear and its visual structure reflects the opaque, circuitous, and disconnected routes and exchanges of capital's commodity chain. Footnotes in Roman numerals carry visual weight and emphasize certain words or ideas, but do not serve their traditional purpose. They grow larger as the text progresses, seemingly laden down with meaning.

Written in its final stages standing up over a sleepless three days, *Topsoil* is a work born of process. In a manner reminiscent of performance artists such as Marina Abramović, Bissen subjected her body and mind to immense strain. Her physicality served as the conduit for her intellectual outpouring, figuratively walking her from New York City back to her former home in the Guatemalan countryside as she wrote. The resulting text continues to evolve as an online commentary that invites critique and response—essentially extending *Topsoil* into new directions.[1]

Bissen, a ruralist, cites artists and theorists such as Abramović, David Harvey, Henri Lefebvre, and Hans Haacke in her discussion of contemporary economic systems of exchange. Conversations with her father, a farmer, were also an important source of inspiration made evident in the text's central focus on soil. Bissen's overarching concern with representation—one of the most resonating themes in *Topsoil*—also positions her work in relation to Guy Debord's *Society of the Spectacle*[2] and Jean Baudrillard's *Simulacra and Simulation*[3]—each of which share a similar fundamental assertion that human experience is now merely the simulation of reality.

For Bissen, "the eyes are passive. But labor is active."[4] Moving beyond the topsoil or the "surface layer" to the substantive soil below is potentially agentive.[5] However, if we are merely looking at the symbols and messages contained in the commodities prescribed for us, then we are not seeing at all. In other words, we have to challenge capital—and the flow of information in the media—on a fundamental level by taking on the very symbols it employs to order our lives.

Topsoil's next phase is in the transition from theory to practice. The work and its growing online commentaries seek out what Bissen refers to as "the spaces of contradiction [that] expose the cracks in the surface."[6] She charts a collective approach to the creation of new meaning within the commodity chain: "1. Start from a representation 2. Find what is [hidden] 3. Represent in a new way what we found."[7]

This text originally appeared in volume III of the *Journal of Biourbanism*.

Art in the Time of Neoliberalism

Stefano Serafini

"Art is about passing through a wall, isn't it?"[1]

"We did not go on television to announce our discoveries. We did not seek grants from academic foundations or praise from the newspaper intellectuals. We brought fuel to the fire."[2]

I met Sara Bissen, my future author, co-writer, wife, and mother of my daughter at a workshop on biourbanism and the state of emergency in Crete in 2014. We talked about her manuscript, *Topsoil*, almost immediately. She agreed to let me read it, despite "nobody ever has." At times, Sara seemed to oscillate from distressed to daydreaming under the heat of those sunny days and the roar of the cicadas. But I could not stop listening to her as she kept talking about subjects that sounded alien to me—rurality, soil, debt, pesticide. Coming from a family of farmers in the United States, she experienced three years of life in rural Guatemala before going to a leftist university in New York City. She then went to Turkey, where she passed through the Gezi uprising in Istanbul. There, she eventually struggled to support her independent research by working as a language teacher. Was she refusing a world that she did not like? I later came to know that she had more than USD 100,000 of college debt on her back. Was she suffering from post-debt stress disorder, like so many young United States citizens who had been coerced into buying a useless consumable called higher education at a high price? There must exist a psychology of debt, the effect of an everyday marketing push into buying its reality—hence, a neurosis convincing people that life cannot help but pay its energetic debt to death. In the end, capitalism is based on a spell or hypnosis, lies we tell ourselves to keep believing we are real if we race like rats. In fact, this hypnosis makes us less real as it plunges our bodies into a dream of slavery. The anarchic force of nonsensical and void rulers comes from this, and the old *novus ordo saeclorum* spell comes true.

The spectacular organization of non-life, this authentic non-dead entirely rules our entropic economy of scarcity and debt. It does not know any finality, let alone any redemptive release (such as the ancient Israeli jubilee that cancelled all debts every 50 years). Capital is not strategic. Indeed, its entire system spins around the absence of value—well signified by the fiat money United States dollar—like a huge vortex-shaped attractor in the space of self-transcending capitalistic phases. The closer to this void people run, the more they agonize, paler and paler, eventually turning into bloodless phantoms.

> …never before has a system of tyranny maintained its lackeys, its experts, and its court jesters so shabbily. They work overtime in the service of emptiness, and emptiness rewards them with coinage in its own image. This is the first time that poor people have imagined themselves to be part of an economic elite, despite all the evidence to the contrary.[3]

Topsoil is neither a dream nor a daydream, but it certainly represents a suspension in time— an absence of reality that calls for the absolute truth of soil and the absolute lie of finance. In a certain way, this odd essay of political economy contradicts the idea that

> debts were warnings of the ultimate truth, they were signs, not yet insistent, of the final inhospitality of life on this earth.[4]

Facing a meaningless, unlimited, financial semiosis and its creation (as a reflection) of signs from signs, soil was introduced by Sara Bissen as the epiphany of the absent structure—the gift that cannot be equated by any exchange. While consumption consumes the substance of our desire, *Topsoil*, with its absence, is the irreparable death or the missing, original jubilee that terminates the system forever.

Sara accepted to publish *Topsoil* under two conditions: no edits, no sale. So our tiny publishing house launched a very complex text without touching a comma and even refused the chance to sell it. The resulting tactic was a piece of a situationist action art, advertised as follows:

> You want to buy Topsoil?
> Fuck you!
> It's not for sale.
> However, if you want to read Topsoil—get in touch.[5]

The book took the form of a five-meter scroll that simulated the depth of soil. Indeed, it had an ISBN code and, as such, a price. But the price was USD 103,159.49 (EUR 84,540.23 at the time), equivalent to Sara's graduate student loans (the rest of her undergradate loans was still being deferred, accruing interest). So much had it cost her to purchase the product of academic education whose output was *Topsoil*.

> Topsoil is the culmination and representation of the author's labor during graduate school. In buying Topsoil, you pay for not only the original, physical copy of the text—you also pay for the reproduction of its labor in relation to the land of Topsoil.[6]

The Italian Publishers Association called me as they had noticed "a mistake" while reviewing *Topsoil*'s ISBN submission. I had to explain that the price was correct. The representative answered: "I see. This must be a very rare, unique book. I'm going to check it out." Indeed, contemporary art can create value out of nothing, following in the footsteps of the scam of the cyclically bursting global financial bubbles and the (so far) USD 88,000 billion of every national debt (worth almost 1 billion copies of *Topsoil*). All it takes is a clerical expert to declare that a certain piece of art is valuable, and the art market carousel (museums, academia, media, politicians, and, very rarely, the artist, too) yields on a new bookkeeping entry while the piece of art enters a bank vault. *Topsoil* indicates that such a carousel is the model of a "real" debt that provides for fake products, such as college education. It is the same poison that seeps into the ground of all the land of the world, providing for the huge rise of farmer suicide and the end of life on this planet. The fact that *Topsoil* can be obtained for free aims to show a way out of this hell.

Sara launched her book at the University of Westminster in London. She brought two copies that ended up stolen within two hours of the presentation. So far, nobody has bought

Topsoil (but several people have asked for it and received it for free in electronic format and, mysteriously, hard copies reached Seattle, Washington, D.C., New York City, Naples, Westphalia, London, Istanbul, Barcelona, and Moscow). Of note, David Harvey did not answer a proposal to bury his book, *Seventeen Contradictions and the End of Capitalism*[7] along with *Topsoil* somewhere in Istanbul.

Neoliberalism is an intentional status rather than a matter of facts. The extermination of even the meaning of the commons, i.e. any relation and object—not to mention nature—abundantly shows it. Representation, political claims, any form of public denunciation, and art not only follow this rule but also constitute the vertebrae of its backbone. Total institutionalization, i.e. institutionalizing the unruly, leads to total subsumption. This is why the subject of *Topsoil* brings in a sacrifice. Sacrifice—and here we deal with a soil sacrifice—is the only real opposite of any spell and the zero point of any significance. *Topsoil*'s total abandonment makes it untamable.

Ten years later, we decided to make *Topsoil* available via the only way that is comprehensible today, i.e. by selling it. But selling means destroying it. Hence, *This Is Not Topsoil. Topsoil* kills itself and leaves a legacy.[8]

If the Renaissance perspective has exemplified and sealed the birth of the individual over the ashes of a society of the commons par excellence (the Middle Ages, where both reality and its principle were commonly acknowledged), then egotism is the escape point of any form of relation in the time of neoliberalism. No matter the pretense of subject, meaning, or goal—there is only one goal, one meaning, and one mobile subject of any form of relation, expression, utterance, and, of course, "art," "politics," and "consumption." This is the compulsion to repeat the representation of the schizo-ego, *la valeur*.

> Value is residue. It is the discourse of signification, our language governed by linguistics. The economy of signification and communication, where we produce and exchange terms and meaning-values, under the law of the code, rests on everything that has not been seized by the symbolic operation of language, by symbolic extermination.[9]

Like Karl Marx, Sara Bissen recognizes François Quesnay rather than Adam Smith as the father of political economy. Soil is the value (the primary matter that capital transforms into fictitious signs of value) and the meaning that flows into any structure like the water of Thales of Miletus. Residual value (finance, debt fractional reserve, art) substitutes the real (rurality, life economy, body, soil), killing it—so to speak—from the inside.

This Is Not Topsoil

*Nothing is sadder than having to beg for existence and
returning naked among the others.*

Jean Baudrillard

1

Topsoil simulates_{xxxiii} soil.

Topsoil[1] is a photograph of a vanishing absence. It is nothing but a trace of a moment in time: a suicide beneath the commodification of everything. Captured, preserved, *Topsoil* is the sign of soil. With *This Is Not Topsoil*, *Topsoil* disappears.

The sign takes you into the disappearance. *This Is Not Topsoil* follows the traces of *Topsoil* and erases them.[2] In doing so, by denying *Topsoil*, it reasserts soil as the anti-sign. Soil is the death that cannot be bought.

We are seduced by a thread, a relic. Soil sounds through a vanished trace.

This is all about the language of soil.

2

Today's world is governed by signs as the future detaches from its linguistic roots. The search for a language of soil is the search for a universal exchange that is based on neither signs nor credit.

The image controls production. Choices seep into the soil. Individual decisions make us vicious participants in a society blinded by an invisible, hidden motive. Human needs and scarcity on the market offer a steady non-euphoria. Enlightened by desires, consumers do what they want, grasping traces in the emptiness.

Buying and selling is in the act of deception.

3

The soil and the farmer are made into a new, exclusive[ccxcv] economic transaction.

New York City, USA – January 29, 2013 noon
It's as if soil is everywhere but nowhere. I decide to look for it anyway.

In politics class, I'm asked to explore a reality through the lens of distance, deceit, and denial. Soil must be longing to be found.

New York City's garment district becomes my subject. An urban industry denies its source. This was never meant to be an ethnography.

I want to borrow nothing.

New York City – March 12, 2013 noon
The garment industry is tied to the fields of cotton in India.

I want to trace a raw material: cotton. I want to

trace it along a commodity chain. And I want to trace the history of soil.

Did you know that farmers are killing themselves?

Washington, D.C., USA – March 26, 2013 2:23 p.m.
I'm sitting next to a farmer on a bus, so I ask him what he thinks of the city.

It smells.

I listen to the ground. If I breathe into soil, will it make a sound? Can I feel it move?

I keep looking for soil. But I don't see my debt looking for me.

New York City – April 9, 2013 noon
Academic writing is sanitized. In fact, it looks a lot like writing for the military. Let's call it mainstream scholarly writing.

Industry comes from war? It's meant for killing. War adapts to diversify its market. Peace maintains war chemical plants for products like fertilizers, pharmaceuticals, and textiles. We overproduce war for everyday things to be used by private citizens.

Break the tendency. Don't write like the military.
And if you crash and burn, at least explain what
you tried to do.

The gate is open. Everyone will take the chance, for sure.

New York City – April 30, 2013 noon
Farmer suicide in India? It's not true. Farmer suicide misrepresents what's going on. It has nothing to do with soil! What are the reasons for farmer suicide? What thread ties it to your narrative? You need a reason to write one. How exactly do you trace soil throughout history? What are you trying to do? Let the narrative speak for itself.

What do you mean by soil? Just deal exclusively with cotton.

This is why you don't let students do open form. The battle is to establish order. You need structuring control.

Soil is interesting. There's an association between darkness and growing things, being commodified. Keep going, but why do you need soil?

Soil doesn't just vanish into thin air, even if that's a thought people want to buy.

New York City – May 4, 2013 6:54 p.m.
The only escape from a hyper-civilized freedom of choice is a suicide wrapped in denial.

The farmer, like the hostage, can be exchanged and liquidated.[1] The farmer-suicide-which-did-not-take-place[2] goes beyond an all-consuming urban world. Buying into a newly packaged society presents itself without shame.

And deceit? Is it even needed?

Isn't it land that you're really talking about?

No, it's about land in relation to labor and capital.

So you have a representation issue.

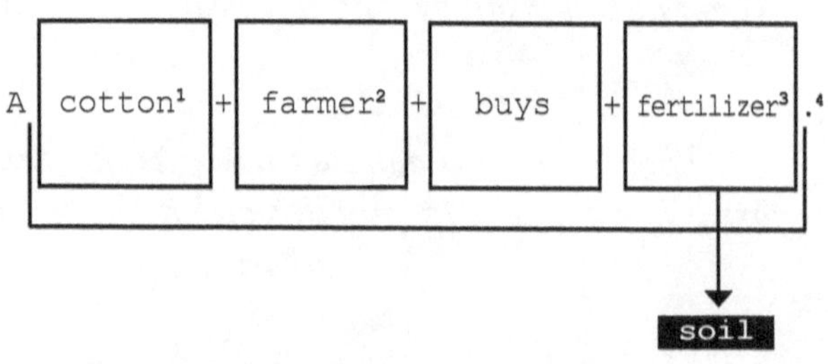

The sentence is a system that forms a layer of topsoil.

Cotton has footnote number 1. Talk about capital in that footnote, in the soil.

The farmer is labor. Another footnote.

Buys is an act that mediates the relationship between the farmer and the fertilizer. It changes everything.

Fertilizer goes into the land. Footnote number 3 takes the reader directly into the soil beneath the layer of topsoil. Through *buys*, the farmer enters the land to be transformed by it.

It even looks like soil—the death that can't be bought.

New York City – May 14, 2013 1:45 a.m.
I'm closer to soil than debt.

One sentence, one fragment threads to the next, word by word, like an embedded undercurrent.

Could it be that soil is looking for me?

New York City – May 14, 2013 8:59 p.m.
I bike across the Manhattan Bridge until I reach the first patch of dirt that I can find. My body burns with the system fully accumulated in it. I sit, and all of the signs that swirl inside of me seep into the ground. Soil is the zero.

New York City – May 15, 2013 4:08 p.m.
My consumption of education catches up to me.
I've chosen to enter a system that comes to a
halt, so I start to borrow time.

I dig for soil, day and night. It fills my thoughts,
my body, the city. What does debt want with
me anyway? Erase me? Transform me into
something else? It has already killed.

My morning alarm goes off. I hear it in the late
afternoon. The entire day slips away, caving in
on itself.

New York City – May 17, 2013 2:10 p.m.
Get your F, and we'll talk.

It seems that there's nothing worth appropriating
here. At least I can try to make soil look real.

New York City – May 18, 2013 5:00 a.m.
Art is about passing through a wall, isn't it?

When it rains, soil weeps and a scent oozes
through the walls of a house. If it's soil that I left
behind, then I must find it. I spend two sleepless
nights walking to it. My legs become red and
swollen as whiskey and coffee keep me awake.

Find the thread from a pulse. Pull it, and it unravels. There's a parallel between myself and what I portray.

I wait for stores to open across the city. Fast fashion lends me clean clothes for the day. With credit, anything is possible.

New York City – May 19, 2013 11:45 p.m.
Three sleepless nights with silence. I stand. I kneel. I'm the only one left in the building. Finals are over. "Open 24 hours" is about to expire.

There's no more space. It now seems that time is worth nothing.

The school wants to close its doors for the night. But I'm still working.

I won't tell anyone you're here,

whispers the janitor.

Can topsoil hide soil forever?

New York City – May 19, 2013 midnight
Security finds me in the last of my clean clothes, a black dress. And my debt? Has it found me, too?

I beg to stay, but it seems I've borrowed too much.

The topsoil begins to break.

On Fifth Avenue, 25 blocks and two avenues from the garment district, I pack my things and bike to the nearest open-for-24-hours school. A sign on the door reads: Closed for graduation. In a tunnel of darkness, I leave Manhattan for my apartment. The night breeze is sweet. I can tell you that, for a moment, soil was here but debt was absent.

New York City – May 20, 2013 1:00 a.m.
Turns out my computer software is older than the school's. My footnote system sinks into my words of soil. This was meant to be an excavation.

The system collapses so that I can see it. It's now 5:33 a.m., and my sleepless eyes meet the gold rising from the darkness.

All that's left is my search for soil.

New York City – May 20, 2013 noon
I'm back at school, alone in the same room.

My work is 24 hours late.

Send it. You're done.

We have plans to go to the beach. I try to rent a car, but can't. It's my birthday, and my driver's license has just expired.

New York City – May 20, 2013 12:18 p.m.
My traces of a cotton commodity chain will be refused, but I submit it anyway.

Unfinished, I call it *Topsoil.*

There's nothing excessive with soil.

Istanbul, Turkey – May 30, 2013 11:30 p.m.
The city is a space of contradictions.

Come to the gathering in Gezi Park.

Topsoil is particularly noteworthy among mainstream scholarly papers and narratives:

Sara Bissen's experimental writing explores the possibilities for imbricating form and substantive argument. This paper rewards close attention to its highly complex structure.

Istanbul – May 31, 2013 5:00 a.m.

Structure is determined by observing the soil in place or by noticing the particles that result from gently shaking or agitating a small quantity of soil.[3]

The occupation tents in the park are burned by the police.

Istanbul – June 1, 2013 9:45 p.m.
The city's spaces are filled with a noxious tear gas.

I still can't see the debt that's after me.

Istanbul – June 2, 2013 10:30 a.m.
There are few places to hide. We're tired of sitting, watching, doing nothing, and feeling ashamed.

I focus less on the urbanization of the countryside than the ruralization of the city. Let's call it the mud of the rural in the urban.

You have some kind of ideology, and I don't know what it is!

A revolution of communities fills cities with difference.

Istanbul – June 3, 2013 11:20 a.m.
The city is produced.

> *Gezi isn't just about a park. It's about capitalism, neoliberalism.*

> *People love their soil. They don't want oppression and darkness.*

I owe debt nothing, even if it has followed me here.

Istanbul – June 15, 2013 2:13 p.m.
> *We want our villages back.*

> *We're brothers and sisters when it comes to production, but not when it comes to distribution.*

Things look the same without soil. This way, white-collar academics can say that nobody cares about the rural.

Istanbul – July 12, 2013 11:10 a.m.
> *When very small areas of two or more kinds of soil are so intricately mixed that it is not feasible to map them separately, they are delineated together, and the resulting combination of soils is called a complex.*[4]

New inhabitants arrived to the village. But the
soil was different, so they left.

Debt can't hear soil.

Istanbul – July 28, 2013 6:34 p.m.
What changes soil? What transforms cotton
into a garment?

We just came from the nice fashion center in
Fatih. Now we're passing it's rural area—rural,
meaning slums.

Newark, New Jersey, USA – October 2, 2013 9:21 a.m.
Accumulation leaves sediments.

Newark – January 12, 2014 3:56 p.m.
I enter vacancy. In capturing absence through a
photograph, I find soil. I take it with me.

Even here, the boundaries between urban and
rural peel away and blur. I see the rural enter
through the city's empty parcels of land. Rotting,
corrosive buildings undergo an act of demolition
through decay—like collapsed barns scattered
across the countryside.

In leaving, soil becomes a wasteland for staying.

Newark – February 9, 2014 1:28 p.m.
Things emerge from soil. The logic of capital is exposed.

Unnoticed, soil hides beneath a mechanism of ephemerality.

Everything else is made up. The mechanism weakens itself. Slowly undone, layers dissolve on the surface of a capital-injected vampire.

Soil traverses the absence. Is this the death that can't be bought? What about the escape?

Soil is in my hands. I can't see any debt, but it's here, too.

Newark – March 1, 2014 12:50 a.m.
Soil must come with me, even if it can no longer hide.

Did I end up borrowing everything?

Money fills up everything, not soil. Hyper-civilization exploits different soils, no matter where I go. Is it really that soil is everywhere but nowhere? Soil, whether it leaves or stays, isn't just interrelated—it's cyclical.

Newark – March 22, 2014 6:45 p.m.
In a decaying center, soil restructures life.

>*You need a reason to write a narrative.*

Soil, as an agent, risks being reduced to meaninglessness under the topsoil of life.

Can I still make soil look real? *Topsoil* tries to say that debt can take something toxic instead of soil.

New York City – May 22, 2014 2:30 p.m.
What's left but debt anyway? Its ruins?

The invisible reclaims itself. Soil can't be institutionalized forever.

The city that draws us into its all-consuming center isn't so relevant. There must be a way to keep pouring soil into myself.

Heraklion, Greece – August 10, 2014 8:31 p.m.
Gold soil—for once, I don't have to pay it back.

Soil shares soil, like roots.

Istanbul – August 21, 2014 12:07 a.m.
> *Topsoil must be published.*

Where?

> *Where else? Artena Anarchist Press.*
> *Then we'll open the Topsoil bank.*

> *Topsoil, by the ruralist Sara Bissen, is an essay*
> *about the dispossession of soil and the reproduction*
> *of capitalistic value. It focuses on the rural*
> *condition—the basis of the pyramid on which the*
> *megamachine is founded. The destructive erosion*
> *of such a basis shows the folly of the system and its*
> *mechanism of the division of consciousness, society,*
> *nature, and body.*

> *Topsoil's form is deliberately disruptive. It demands*
> *an effort to match because the form is also a dynamic*
> *of the reality and political/analytical action.*

> *This operation aims at: 1) becoming part of a*
> *work that is more than a mere critical essay but*
> *a political action; a methodological innovation;*
> *an essay; a form of science, and a poetic art—in*
> *the radical sense of* poiein *(doing, in Greek),*
> *and 2) denouncing the particular imposture of*

university debt that feigns a market that does not exist and is in part the more general imposture about never-ending growth. In turn, this is connected to the subject of the book: dispossession based on value production.

Istanbul – October 5, 2014, 6:10 p.m.

One condition: no edits.

Topsoil captures a moment in time. It stays as is, unfinished—as the commodification of education.

Another thing: it's not for sale.

Istanbul – October 26, 2014 10:11 p.m.
Topsoil is a scroll. It was always meant to be read like soil.

It's impressive how we can make things real.

Istanbul – December 16, 2014 7:36 p.m.
Topsoil is bailed out ahead of print. I owe nothing.

From source to product, a commodity chain fragments and contradicts. Soil, with the most agency, transforms an indebted role.

Istanbul – December 20, 2014 10:21 p.m.
The city exists as imagery, as form, as a reproduction of signs and symbols from a historically accumulative past. Objects are perfected when finished. But what about an idea?

Istanbul – January 1, 2015 4:05 p.m.
Topsoil's sale price is set at the debt that finds me here: $103,159.49. Interest accumulates for 1,670 days. If you want to read it, then I share it. *Topsoil* isn't a bank loan, and the collective dialogue around it is a living art form. It aims at generating a place for tearing down the logics of capitalistic representation.

Topsoil is a naked body without the rhetorical make-up. The process is a drama in itself, a Sacra Rappresentazione. *The boxes at the beginning are the chorus—I was lost with them, and intrigued. The text was dense but very clear, rich. The* Narrazione—*I followed it with intentionality. The pulsating, uninterrupted, and tense flow of the discourse was very pleasant—a philosophical pleasure. The original way of exposing stayed a mystery, but a mystery that must have an explication at some layer of the story and didn't disturb the reading. The fragmentation of phrases through punctuation was clear enough. It offered,*

*in emotional and rhythmical terms, the breaking
and destructuring effect of capital over a reality that
is at once, evident, but at the same time subject to
invisibility and decomposition. At the end, there is
the note that explains the methodology and, despite
the cue at the beginning, the theatrical stage becomes
clear: how parts are connected and why, the logic of
layers, the Roman numerals, and the way of quoting/
hiding/revealing. By entering it, one can understand
it; by believing the drama, the ancient Greek could
receive the* katarxis, *the transformative message.*

Istanbul – September 2, 2015 5:18 p.m.
I consider moving again. Stillness is when the
ground takes root.

Artena, Italy – January 15, 2016 2:56 p.m.
*Moving beyond the topsoil or the "surface layer"
to the substantive soil below is potentially
agentive… we have to challenge capital—and
the flow of information in the media—on a
fundamental level by taking on the very symbols
it employs to order our lives.*[5]

Artena – March 9, 2016 8:40 p.m.
The land sees, even if we don't. Soil can be home.

Artena – September 7, 2016 12:21 a.m.
The city smells of decay, and *Topsoil* unfolds
into rurality.

Our words have become empty. It's as if we
no longer inhabit them, as if they're no longer
filled with soil.[6]

Emptiness isn't silence.

Artena – October 19, 2016 2:50 p.m.
*Topsoil's subnotations are distracting. This makes
it hard to read and focus on the content. And no
one can crack the code!*

Artena – April 2, 2017 7:29 a.m.
The society of the spectacle is a lie. The I in the
ruins knows the collapse. The remains of the
rural are within our fleeting urban. Modernity
is a ruthless break that breathes the never-
ending ruptures of its own making. The urban
reproduces and no one can stay. It needs bodies
from the rural. The urban rots the wood. The
urban is made to collapse. The rural condition
changes, but the urban fails to stay.

There is no code, so there is no code to crack.

Artena – July 28, 2018 3:09 p.m.
People need to be attracted to the value of debt.

With no market value, *Topsoil* can never be exchanged for something else. *Topsoil* envy ensues amid a lack of comparison.

Demand must be created.

Artena – July 15, 2019 9:36 p.m.
Words are filled with the silence of soil so that words shine the gold of their denied meaning.[7] Soil is the threshold to Aeneas' golden branch. Through the forest of words and out of the valley of debt.

Artena – August 1, 2019 2:17 p.m.
Debt leaves a residue, even after the accumulation stops. The chance of spiraling backwards risks casting a shadow on life.

Artena – December 30, 2020 2:37 a.m.
This Is Not Topsoil follows *Topsoil.*

Now a trace, *Topsoil* is made into an object. Simulating soil is different than following *Topsoil.*

Topsoil is disorder. *This Is Not Topsoil* is order because the market is inside of us.

Artena – September 1, 2021 10:18 p.m.
This Is Not Topsoil reaches out to the masses. It's going to be a book for sale. People buy books, not scrolls.

Topsoil wasn't really for sale, so it was never real.

The market will make *This Is Not Topsoil* look real.

Artena – October 1, 2021 6:02 p.m.
Topsoil is removed from its original, institutionalized context and restored. Art doesn't really pass through a wall. *This Is Not Topsoil* grasps that thread.

Artena – October 22, 2021 5:48 p.m.
In *This Is Not Topsoil*, the word *artist* is filled with what it was meant to be: *persona*.

Persona sounds through—from behind the mask, from the soil.

Self-declared artist imagery doesn't do this. Neither does debt.

Fake (finance, art) ruins the real (soil, reality).

Artena – November 3, 2021 9:30 a.m.
Artists are tourists who pretend to be inhabitants. They stem from a non-society where work turns into deceit. They use their own consumerism to feed consumption.

This happens when people have nothing to say and can only show.[8] As tourists, artists fade reality into their own immateriality, creating the exchange value of floating, rootless ideas and things.

Soil isn't about fakery, and artists are shameless in not erasing their footsteps.

Artena – December 6, 2021 3:23 a.m.
The city is the necropolis. Contemporary art is all about finance.[9] Distance is valuable for both, and both tools dictate a disappearance and how far that disappearance goes. It's discordant—like war. Culture, as we know it, is just a representation of value. It imitates life. Fashion, marketing, and design try to make "the art world" real so that abstractions, reductions, and mirrors form the society in which we live. And artists fashion themselves above the market, beyond

buying and selling. It's a commodity trick, like pulling farmers into the market.

Artists let finance pay as they play the agent. Art museums are dead anarchic supermarkets. There will be no more peasants, no rural. This is how you create value out of nothing.

> *Do what you can with someone else's debt.*

The artist leaves, and the word *fertilizer* stays.

Artena – January 3, 2022 10:16 a.m.
> *Soil needs lethal aid. Let's send it.*

Fertilizer is thought of as a productive, generative agent that's "good" enough to buy, so farmers buy it. Synthetic and meant to enhance, fertilizer consumes both the farmer and the soil. Farmers in India ingest their own pesticide to escape the shame of debt.

Pesticide, in fact, reflects the tragic reality of farmer suicide. But I want to convey a connection between fertilizer and pesticide. Liquid fertilizer, as a sign of progress and deceit, turns against both humans and nature.

Fertilizer, as a chemical input, is the interaction of debt beneath the topsoil.

Here, consumption is consumed. All of this is denied with ease.

Artena – January 19, 2022 9:28 a.m.
This Is Not Topsoil discards heavy remnants of an older footnote system. Certain fragments and breaks remain in a vanished absence.

This Is Not Topsoil follows *Topsoil* and erases it.

Artena – May 1, 2022 7:46 p.m.
Soil is full of silence, and silence makes space for words to sound through.

4

<code>Watch</code>_{clxviii} `the topsoil erode.`

Progress is death and that is the starting point.

The disappearance of *Topsoil* means that soil needs to die for progress. Life can only be exchanged on a level of value that the sign can comprehend. But soil knows where to go—it cannot be reproduced. Death is the limit that capital cannot exchange.

Signs and the exchange of goods dislocate society. The resulting form and content rest on precarity. Do we recognize our own absence in soil? The representation of value is fictitious.[1] But how much fiction can we bear? An unraveling rurality is the first to expose a system that is being torn apart at the seams.

A deadly system forges ahead without any individual. Scarcity and death are repeated and consumed.[2] Life, lost to subordination, keeps us all in debt. Life and death are one in soil. The decayed city enters a rural that invites a new future.

5

This is the point of rupture[lx].

A substratum emerges from the shattering and collapse of a system. The rural can elucidate otherwise hidden relations that emerge and recede throughout processes of making people urban. This lens shows the need to establish the peripheries as a new form of center for a future that goes beyond capitalism. It involves a strategy of survival and patterns of adaptation of the rural, meant as a general anthropological category within an urban world and worldview.

The linguistic root of soil details what the modern anthropological category of the rural from the so-called peripheries means for our Western and westernized world, which we tend to identify as urban. Take, for example, Italy, the site of production for *This Is Not Topsoil*. Italy, once a largely rural economy, plays an industrial, post-war role in the West as the most advanced front for both revolution and counter-revolution.[1]

As an exemplary scene, Italy is a special laboratory where the clashes and transformations happening all over the Western world occur in similar forms and different nuances. The country's rapid transition from a pre-industrial anthropology to a modern lifestyle was viewed as an economic "miracle" and became a distinguishing feature of Italian society. Pier Paolo Pasolini, an Italian poet and acute observer, left one of the deepest and richest accounts on those years, especially the post-war boom that transformed a mainly rural country into a consumeristic society. This extends into the events of 1968 and Italy's Years of Lead, which represent the relics of Pasolini's time.

With his continual reference to what Ernesto De Martino called *età del pane* (the age of bread) and the Souths of the world (a transnational pre-capitalist reality of peasantry and sub-proletariats),[2] Pasolini provided a key thread in understanding what I call the language of soil. Understanding this language is vital, and his insight into the rural world of the 20th-century peasant and sub-proletariat is a testament within his own artistic and intellectual world.

Fast forward and we see that today's progressive, techno-centric, and finance-based globalism of the 21st century has little to offer the rural. Used (and misused) for production yet barely tolerated, the rural is at the antithesis of the direction pursued by our society. At the same time, the traces of its central, almost mythological character—the peasant—appears opposite to the man of the future. Why turn toward this world—let alone something like soil, which is at the core of it?

Teodor Shanin articulated that peasantry is a relevant process with its own economic, social, and historical identity.[3] This process bleeds into an expolary economy that represents the emerging tip of a complex anthropological alternative to capitalism. Norbert Elias analyzed the civilizing process as an attempted eradication of peasantry under modern state capitalism[4] and, during the 20th century, John Berger wrote about this anthropology.[5] There is a need to see the risk in liquidating rural qualities and how this part of society may, in fact, represent a way toward the future of a world that has abandoned this linguistic root.

The search for the language of soil within the transcultural transformation of the rural aims to illuminate a post-urban anthropology where the syntax of soil is the root of non-consumption. Myths, symbols, and relations make this transnational, pre-capitalist world alive in the physical, social, and conceptual reality of the rural world. It is about opposing the anti-sign of soil against today's reign of signs. The language of soil is needed for more than navigating and surviving our largely urban times. Without such an understanding, this world, embodied by soil, risks perishing in what Berger refers to as the final act of historical elimination.[6]

Soil hides, and *Topsoil* vanishes.

NOTES

We See Only What Has Been Produced for Us to See

1. Bissen, S. (2015). Topsoil lxiii. http://topsoillxiii.com

2. Debord, G. (1967). *La société du spectacle* [Society of the Spectacle]. Paris: Éditions Buchet-Chastel.

3. Baudrillard, J. (1981). *Simulacres et simulation* [Simulacra and Simulation]. Paris: Éditions Galilée.

4. Bissen, S. (2015). *Topsoil*. Artena: Artena Anarchist Press, 4, [cxxxii] and [ccxv] (after Lefebvre).

5. Ibidem, 4, [i].

6. Ibidem, 3, [lxxii].

7. Ibidem, 4, [xxix].

Art in the Time of Neoliberalism

1. Bissen, S. (2024). *This Is Not Topsoil*. Artena: Artena Anarchist Press, p. 10.

2. Debord, G. (1978). *IN GIRUM IMUS NOCTE ET CONSUMIMUR IGNI*. (K. Knabb, Trans.). The Anarchist Library, p. 11. https://theanarchistlibrary.org/library/guy-debord-in-girum-imus-nocte-et-consumimur-igni.pdf

3. Ibidem, p. 3.

4. Berger, J. (1987). *Once in Europa*. New York: Vintage International, p. 53.

5. Bissen, S. (2015). Topsoil lxiii. Buy. In: https://topsoillxiii.com/buy-topsoil/
6. Ibidem.

7. Harvey, D. (2014). *Seventeen Contradictions and the End of Capitalism*. New York: Oxford University Press.

8. Borselli, S. (2011). Senza eredità. Il tema della trasmissione dei beni di famiglia in R. M. Rilke e G. Debord, con un'ipotesi sul suicidio del secondo [Without inheritance: On the transmission of family assets in R. M. Rilke and G. Debord, with a hypothesis on the latter's suicide]. *Il Covile*, No. 658. Florence. www.ilcovile.it/scritti/COVILE_658_Rilke_Debord.pdf

9. Baudrillard, J. (1993 [1976]). *Symbolic Exchange and Death*. (I. Hamilton Grant, Trans.). London: SAGE Publications, p. 200.

This Is Not Topsoil

1

1. Bissen, S. (2015). *Topsoil*. Artena: Artena Anarchist Press.

2. Calle, S. & Baudrillard, J. (1988 [1983]). *Suite vénitienne/Please Follow Me*. (D. Barash & D. Hatfield, Trans.). Seattle: Bay Press.

3

1. Baudrillard, J. (1995). *The Gulf War Did Not Take Place*. (P. Patton, Trans.). Bloomington: Indiana University Press.

2. Bissen, S. (2020). Yes, U.S. farmer suicide is significantly higher than the national average. *Organisms: Journal of Biological Sciences*, 4(1):17–25, doi:10.13133/2532-5876/16959

3. United States Department of Agriculture (1961).

Soil Survey of Shelby County, Iowa (Series 1956, no. 16). Washington, D.C.: USDA, p. 3.

4. Ibidem.

5. Nosari, K. (2015). We see only what has been produced for us to see. *Journal of Biourbanism*, *III*(1&2):91–92.

6. Bissen, S. (2016). Editor's note. *Journal of Biourbanism*, *IV*(1&2):7–11.

7. Bissen, S. (2020). A forest of words. *Journal of Biourbanism*, *VIII*(1):105–106.

8. Pasolini, P. P. (2008 [1975]). 7 gennaio 1973. Il «discorso» dei capelli [January 7, 1973: The "Discourse" on Long Hair]. In: *Scritti corsari* [Corsair Writings], pp. 5–11. Milan: Garzanti Editore.

9. Graeber, D. (2011). The sadness of post-workerism. In: *Revolutions in Reverse: Essays on Politics, Violence, Art, and Imagination*, pp. 79–105. London: Minor Compositions.

4

1. Polanyi, K. (2001). *The Great Transformation: The Political and Economic Origins of Our Time*. Boston: Beacon Press.

2. Bissen, S. (2015). *Topsoil*. Artena: Artena Anarchist Press.

5

1. Debord, G. (1992 [1967]). *La società dello spettacolo* [Society of the Spectacle]. (P. Salvadori, Trans.). Milan: Baldini Castoldi Dalai.

2. Pasolini, P. P. (2008 [1975]). 8 luglio 1974. Limitatezza

della storia e immensità del mondo contadino [July 8, 1974: Limitedness of the history and immensity of the peasant world]. In: *Scritti corsari* [Corsair Writings], pp. 51–55. Milan: Garzanti Editore.

3. Shanin, T. (1990). *Defining Peasants: Essays Concerning Rural Societies, Expolary Economies, and Learning from Them in the Contemporary World*. Oxford: Basil Blackwell.

4. Elias, N. (2000 [1939]). *The Civilizing Process: Sociogenetic and Psychogenetic Investigation*s. E. Dunning, J. Goudsblom, & S. Mennell (Eds.). (E. Jephcott, Trans.). Malden, MA: Blackwell Publishing.

5. See *Into Their Labours*, a trilogy by John Berger on Europe's 20th-century peasant eclipse: Berger, J. (1979). *Pig Earth*. New York: Pantheon Books; Berger, J. (1987). *Once in Europa*. New York: Vintage International; Berger, J. (1990). *Lilac and Flag: An Old Wive's Tale of a City*. London: Granta Books. See also, on contemporary "urban peasantry," Neuwirth, R. (2006). *Shadow Cities: A Billion Squatters, A New Urban World*. New York: Routledge.

6. Berger, J. (1979). *Pig Earth*. New York: Pantheon Books, p. 213. See also Lindqvist, S. (1996 [1992]). *"Exterminate All the Brutes"*. (J. Tate, Trans.). London: Granta Books, which exposes the brutality of modern exploitation by tracing the roots of the West's thirst for imperial slaughter to the Holocaust on its own soil.

[This Is Not]
TOPSOIL

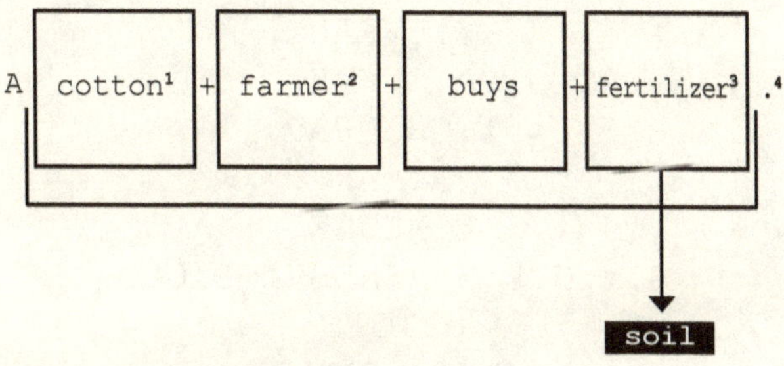

A
cotton[1]
+ farmer[2]
+ buys
+ fertilizer[3]
.[4]
soil

CHARACTERS
IN ORDER OF APPEARANCE

R.BEELEVF
F.Z.FERIGEWINKEIZCO
Y.EVRAH
A.CHEAK
I.CHATPAR
R.MAX
L.NEUGE
G.N.N.P.HVAINDBVAMDIORO
C.TOTS
Ć.MAROVAIB
V.E.SWENJIAKH
S.BIENS

ACT ONE

A cotton[1] farmer[2] buys fertilizer[3].[4]

[1] Cotton[i] is a commodity. Cotton comes from a seed[ii]. A cottonseed is placed into the ground by a farmer[iii].

[2] The cotton farmer[i] works a terrain that is governed (R.Beelevf). The farmer uses a single instrument to plow a field[ii] (R.Beelevf). Many instruments of labor[iii] unite on a factory floor, where a factory worker uses scissors, pins, needles, and a sewing machine to stitch one piece of fabricated cotton to another piece of fabricated cotton (R.Beelevf). Labor tools are administered by a division[iv] of labor (R.Beelevf). Workers who use these instruments are also administered[v] by a division of labor (R.Beelevf). Cotton, as a commodity, becomes a chain[vi] designed to guarantee movements of labor, even if the location of work

never moves (R.Beelevf + Y.Evrah). Movement of cotton[vii] (R.Beelevf). Movement of fibers[viii] (R.Beelevf). Movement of thread, movement of patterns[ix] (R.Beelevf). The city, the administrator of power, divides cotton flows[x] into multiple, varying sectors to ensure the maintenance of a proper labor operative and direct multiple, varying flows of values that originate from cotton (R.Beelevf). From the farmer, located in a cotton field in India, to the consumer, located in a shop in New York City, cotton manifests as a t-shirt, where everyone who touches[xi] cotton manifests as an instrument within the larger urbanized cotton mechanism (R.Beelevf). Change happens in the exchange from one hand[xii] to another (R.Beelevf). Cotton travels directly from point [a] to[xiii] point [b] (F.Z.Ferigewinkeizco). The direction from [a] to [b] is near-sighted[xiv], but this deficit is concealed by the change of hands from one [cotton farmer] to the spatially nearest yet farthest in the commodity chain [consumer of cotton], depending on who or what is closest to the cotton farmer. The transformation[xv] of cotton is facilitated by a process of changing hands from one farmer to one consumer, divided across divided time and divided locations (F.Z.Ferigewinkeizco). The workers enveloped in that space[xvi] live and work within individual workboxes led by the sequence and vision of one, single commodity chain of cotton (F.Z.Ferigewinkeizco). A change of hands and a change of focus attempts to eliminate difference[xvii] from things that are different (F.Z.Ferigewinkeizco). There is a complexity between[xviii] cotton farmers and cotton buyers, from cotton sellers and back to cotton farmers, which exists at every single turn in the exchange of, and in the relations of, cotton (F.Z.Ferigewinkeizco). Re-enacted[xix] by every farmer, banker, seed seller, factory worker, fabric cutter, patternmaker, urban planner, real estate developer, and consumer (R.Beelevf). However, the concept of a commodity chain does not automatically demand a labor of divisional geographies[xx] between the cotton fields in India and the storefronts in New York City. Nor automatically demand a self-disciplining distributional system for the products of labor based on a mutually agreed upon hybrid[xxi] (F.Z.Ferigewinkeizco). Everything within one cotton commodity chain interrelates[xxii] and overlaps. The exchange of one cotton farmer's knowledge[xxiii] for a packaged product can be traced by following points along a map, in every corner that cotton touches (Y.Evrah). The farthest point is found by standing in the center of a cotton field and locating the highest concentration[xxiv] of workers who possess a specialization, therefore predicting the value of their time and space. Possession of a "special"-ization[xxv] backs all workers, reliant on cotton field experts, against a wall (R.Beelevf). Specialization along the cotton chain allows[xxvi] new cotton farmers to enter it; they are situated and adhered[xxvii] to their place of work with limited mobility. They risk being nothing but a moving[xxviii] link in a cotton commodity chain that is disguised as a cotton labor community (R.Beelevf). This progressive line functions by permitting entrance[xxix] to or exclusion from what can or cannot belong to a backwards past, based on a cotton farmer's ability to abandon a natural way of life for a synthetic fiber (R.Beelevf). The multiple layers[xxx] of complexity that such a life possesses is denied, along with any tracings of its prior dirty processes. Nothing disappears[xxxi] completely (R.Beelevf). The work reproduced[xxxii] in the commodified cotton chain contains a specific representation of a life without Earth: a specific imaginary of work, a living that detaches[xxxiii] itself; a detachment that operates as unsocially necessary[xxxiv] labor used to reproduce new modalities in the garment and fashion industry in New York City; a work tailored for the right type, the right size, and the right kind[xxxv] of labor, distanced from any other processes (R.Max).

The garment manufacturing industry in New York City is drawn up, fit, cut, and justified[xxxvi] by an assumed worthiness. City buildings are made into a zone[xxxvii] of preservation, created by measuring, cutting, buying, selling, and stitching together the workers who measure, cut, buy, and sell, acting out all of the processes designed to preserve the intelligence and skills needed to measure, cut, buy, and sell one cotton t-shirt to increase the worth of that one cotton t-shirt for anything or anyone who touches that cotton t-shirt. This is where[xxxviii] our gaze is told to look: at the injection[xxxix] of value into one specific, fabricated arrangement of factories and stores that once sat like empty boxes, void of value to justify the worthiness of being saved. What do these buildings produce to make the work created between their walls[xl] so special, so valuable? Oversaturation[xli]. Consumptive[xlii] functions. Advertising and images[xliii] that appear to come from somewhere else, something else (R.Beelevf). A contradiction[xliv] of space. Desire and contempt at once[xlv], in space. Filled and wrapped in a city box with contradictions that are trapped[xlvi] yet exposed. The garment industry is located inside[xlvii] the city, where the city is the most effective tool for making images. It is a living and working representation of space, imagined[xlviii] (R.Beelevf). Pre-packaged[xlix] as commodity. A city wrapped and dressed by, clothed in the value of its surroundings[l]. The reproduction[li] of labor, of people from a cotton plant, is brought to life by the reproduction and collection of products from the farmers who work in the fields of India. The city's roots of contradiction, unlabeled, serve the division, specialization, and accumulation of products, tailor-made for city dwellers who already own the keys to the storage room that contains the master plans[lii] of their city and its use. This preserved zone of specialized labor, which incubates[liii] in specialized buildings in New York City, operates as a daily conflict zone that is rooted between the imbalance of concentrations and voids. It serves[liv] to detach and represent an original work. It serves as a material that hides itself in an empty box[lv]. Beneath the addition of more buildings, more power, more trains, and more streets, specific kinds of extra workers can then add more value to the already empty boxes based on the expected worth[lvi] of a final cotton t-shirt or future store, where a cotton consumer buys a t-shirt. The city is then in a position to dominate and parasitically generate contradiction after contradiction[lvii]. New York City is not the international city we perceive[lviii]. The city holds power[lix]; power is rarely labeled[lx] clearly. Authority divides labor in order to exploit the divisions[lxi] (R.Beelevf). The counter-project to authority stitches together the fragments that are left behind[lxii]. If seeing is all we are capable of doing, then our eyes get distorted, misperceive[lxiii], and even become useless (R.Beelevf). Sight may possess an agency, but we are left with only signs[lxiv] and representations of a perceived reality. Symbols[lxv] of a false unity wind up as mirrors, nothing more — except as another sign, another image (R.Beelevf). The reasons for existence erode[lxvi]. A better[lxvii] word than honour is human dignity (A.Cheak). The latter tends to keep the individual[lxviii] in mind (A.Cheak). If not the latter in mind, then the laborer does not use the tool but serves[lxix] the machine (R.Beelevf). Relationships[lxx] are inside and outside (R.Beelevf). Whatever lies the farthest outside the process dominates[lxxi] (R.Beelevf). And what is outside is the only thing[lxxii] of importance (R.Beelevf). Like how designers see and what is seen from what they see is the only[lxxiii] important thing (R.Beelevf). All other designs, all other processes, are blinded[lxxiv] (R.Beelevf). A use value, that is, not just an exchange value, is like an inside-outside[lxxv] relationship (R.Beelevf). The dominant is[lxxvi] outside. But inside, socially necessary labor[lxxvii] understands what needs to be done and what needs to be understood (Y.Evrah). When a human being[lxxviii] becomes a commodity. As package[lxxix]. When we egoize[lxxx] (L.Neuge + R.Beelevf), we lose the ability to feel nature and can only feel its reproduction (R.Beelevf). As commodity[lxxxi]. Felt instead is whatever is most immediate[lxxxii] (R.Beelevf). In time[lxxxiii]. In location[lxxxiv]. It is difficult to internalize[lxxxv]. The farmers divide[lxxxvi] their work. The farmers$_{lxxxvii}$ divide their time. The farmers divide their home$_{lxxxviii}$. The boundaries between work and life blur$_{lxxxix}$. A single$_{xc}$ farmer. One single cotton$_{xci}$. One single fiber$_{xcii}$. Exists$_{xciii}$. Exists$_{xciv}$. In, within, between, beyond, around, below, above, scattered, and absorbed$_{xcv}$ into a strategic world order (R.Beelevf). Inescapable$_{xcvi}$ from one single power. The individual$_{xcvii}$ who thinks to be independent from and unrelated to the system is deluded (I.Chatpar). As one person, an actor's work lies within$_{xcviii}$ the complexity.

[3] Each single box$_i$ in the cotton commodity chain makes a seamless sequence (R.Beelevf). The sequence passes from checkpoint to checkpoint, where each box is proportionately$_{ii}$ less (R.Beelevf). The boxes pass every point since the uninterrupted sequence appears as an unbroken fiber, evenly weaved into one$_{iii}$. Pieced together in an order, between

New York City and Nagpur, this is the requirement for a seamless reduction to be grasped and finally take root[iv] (R.Beelevf). Beneath the surface, the cottonseed roots into the ground[v] (R.Beelevf). The land is where the seed is sown and where the roots take hold of a complex[vi] ecology (R.Beelevf). Sun, water, and wind support the growth of the cotton plant and act as operating elements in the chain, as a piece of thread of fabric within the final cotton t-shirt[vii] (R.Beelevf). The outside forces that produce a cotton plant[viii] are made invisible within the garment manufacturing industry. This industry cannot be seen[ix] within its epicenter on 38th Street between Eighth and Ninth Avenues. Nothing disappers[x] completely (R.Beelevf). Regulation flows produced by cotton and the cotton farmers emerge from their site-specific origin[xi] into a final, dispossessed destination determined by the same yet opposing site — both of which are defined by land and their use (R.Beelevf + Y.Evrah). Since cotton changes hands based on a division of labor within each location along the commodity chain, from cotton to garment, we find another space of exchange[xii] at each moment in the transformation of cotton: a market of place[xiii] (R.Beelevf). A place that anticipates our attempt to understand[xiv], based on what we perceive, and how we relate to the stores and factories in New York City (R.Beelevf). There is a desire to read[xv] this city, but it can be discouraging so we read something else (R.Beelevf). The contradictions of this place make it difficult to decode[xvi] its images and text (R.Beelevf). One can make an effort to decipher before giving up, before accepting complexity as a given[xvii] and finally decide to scan just the surface. Passivity[xviii] prevents a process of untying the stacked boxes of the city to see what happens in and around a final pile of cotton t-shirts. Denying[xix] the breakdown of these boxes that store cotton t-shirts means that the boxes hold the power to be everything and everywhere at once: hung on racks, untouched, buried in storage basements, and graspable behind spotless[xx] windows (R.Beelevf). Spaces of capital may be able to bury themselves, but the bloodless[xxi] can still capture and kill the living (R.Beelevf). Life is extracted[xxii] from raw materials like cotton (R.Beelevf). Extraction allows the commodity chain, until its end in New York City, to become a lifeless[xxiii] t-shirt that appears alive and valid even if detached from its rooted source: cotton (R.Beelevf). Cotton productivity[xxiv] in India is low (G.N.N.P.Hvainadbvamdioro). The major cotton producing states[xxv] in India are Maharashtra, Gujarat, Andhra Pradesh, Punjab, Karnataka, and Madhya Pradesh (G.N.N.P.Hvainadbvamdioro). Production includes both rainfed and irrigated[xxvi] cotton (G.N.N.P.Hvainadbvamdioro). Cotton in India has been industrialized[xxvii] to enhance productivity (R.Beelevf). This process of industrialization is situated on a piece of land[xxviii]. Capitalist agriculture anticipated the disappearance[xxix] of soil (R.Beelevf). Capitalist agriculture anticipated the disappearance of the cotton farmer[xxx] who works the [soil] (R.Beelevf). The soil and the cotton farmer are distanced[xxxi] from the profit generated by production. There is a shift[xxxii]. Soil is subject[xxxiii] to the demands of capital. Wealth and income are distanced from[xxxiv] cotton. These demands dictate the farmer's situation[xxxv] in life and in work (R.Beelevf). How does the farmer work[xxxvi] the soil (R.Beelevf)? The farmer[xxxvii] is subject to the demands of capital (R.Beelevf). The soil is far[xxxviii] from the garment manufacturing industry in New York City. Here, the industry's demands[xxxix] are fulfilled by cotton production (R.Beelevf). The city reflects the dissolve[xl] of agriculture into industry (R.Beelevf). Agriculture goes to a place where it can be reconstructed, refit, and absorbed[xli]. Nothing disappears[xlii] completely (A.Cheak + R.Beelevf). The life of the farmer is a hidden transcript, where physical[xliii] labor is a medium (C.Tots). One must seek an alternative space[xliv] to perform a public transcript (C.Tots + Ć.Marovaib + R.Beelevf). Such a space produces[xlv] a new territory (Ć.Marovaib). The space produces a new[xlvi] relationship (R.Beelevf). Here, labor[xlvii] can be produced. It is the labor of the *persona* to re-enact, undo[xlviii], redo, and rethink. To act[xlix]. To be the *persona* who performs at the site[l] of tension. The space in between[li]. The friction[lii] of terrain. Friction exposes the tension[liii] in the terrain. The tension between two opposites exposes a contradiction of territory[liv]. Terrain[lv]. Land[lvi]. Capital[lvii]. Soil[lviii]. Spaces of contradiction expose the cracks[lix] in the surface.

This is the point of rupture$_{lx}$. The rupture opens for a logic$_{lxi}$ to emerge from beneath the layers of absolute knowledge. The logic comes from those who touch$_{lxii}$ the soil: the farmer is with the soil$_{lxiii}$. The farmer, with the soil, collides with the absolute and confronts the linear logic of a cotton commodity chain in the shattering$_{lxiv}$ of space. There are places$_{lxv}$ for selling anything and everything along the cotton chain (R.Beelevf). There is a market$_{lxvi}$ for cotton, for the cotton farmer, and for all of the supplies that go into the production of cotton. Surplus value$_{lxvii}$. Profit$_{lxviii}$.

All things extracted$_{lxix}$ from cotton require even distribution (Y.Evrah). Not just money, but anything that unjustly belongs$_{lxx}$ to someone. Labor time$_{lxxi}$ from the soil should belong to the farmer who works the soil. The farmer has a relationship$_{lxxii}$ with the soil. Laborer$_{lxxiii}$. A human being$_{lxxiv}$ in possession of immaterial things. Dignity[lxxv]. Community[lxxvi]. Knowledge[lxxvii]. The soil is constantly induced[lxxviii] by labor (R.Beelevf). A continual turning[lxxix] of soil ties the cotton farmer to the soil (R.Beelevf). Land is immovable[lxxx] (R.Beelevf). The cotton farmers who are tied[lxxxi] to the land are immovable (Y.Evrah). They are tied through a social[lxxxii] process of production (R.Beelevf). A process[lxxxiii] of socially necessary labor; labor that is both social and necessary[lxxxiv]. Labor is measured by time[lxxxv] that is social and necessary. Soil[lxxxvi] needs the cotton farmer. Cotton needs[lxxxvii] the soil. It is intimate and owns[lxxxviii] its own time. The relationship is one of proximity[lxxxix]. The process owns its own sweat and blood[xc], which also belongs to the earth. Labor tied to the earth[xci] is immovable. The earth is an agent of production[xcii] (R.Beelevf + R.Max). Land[xciii] is an agent of production. Soil[xciv] is an agent of production. An agent[xcv] of soil is fertilizer. An agent of the cotton farmer is fertilizer[xcvi]. Fertilizer is a commodity[xcvii]. Labor and soil become[xcviii] a commodity. Fertilizer is an agent of production within[xcix] the soil. Fertilizer is absorbed[c] into the soil complex. The absorption changes[ci] the soil. The structure of the soil complex[cii] shifts. Humans live from[ciii] this structural complex. No matter how far[civ]. Fertilizer seeps deeper[cv] into the soil. Farther[cvi] from the topsoil. Depth counts[cvii] distance within a complex structure, which the fertilizer as agent changes. The soil causes the complex to be broken down into different properties[cviii] that affect the production of cotton. The cotton yield increases[cix]. Farmers decrease[cx]. The fertilizer decomposes[cxi] the farmer's body. Back[cxii] into the land. The fertilizer decomposes[cxiii] soil. Capital[cxiv]. Fertilizer[cxv]. Fertilizer is a commodity in the chain that leads[cxvi] to capital. The commodity chain is broken down[cxvii] into fragments. Not only the soil complex but also the relationships between[cxviii] the soil and the cotton farmer are broken down. This is a spatial[cxix] relationship. A social[cxx] relationship. Soil combined into an area becomes land[cxxi]. Land under state capitalism is enclosed[cxxii]. Land is a parcel[cxxiii]. A parcel is an enveloped[cxxiv] box. The farmer tied[cxxv] to that land is a parcel. Capital dominates[cxxvi] this parcel of land and labor. It is a domination over[cxxvii] the intimacy and proximity of a relationship. Capital is far[cxxviii] from this connection. Due to this distance and disconnect, capital is governed by a separate time and a separate space[cxxix]. A space of absolute power[cxxx] (R.Beelevf). That articulates itself as pure[cxxxi] speculation. Unnatural[cxxxii]. Abstract[cxxxiii]. Absolute power is abstract[cxxxiv] power (R.Beelevf). Fragments[cxxxv]. Soil [and][cxxxvi] labor become fragments. The word *and* is in parentheses[cxxxvii]. Just because this word is in parentheses between two sentences does not remove[cxxxviii] it from the sentence. Nothing[cxxxix] disappears completely (R.Beelevf). Destructive materials have a history of being deposited[cxl] into the soil (R.Beelevf). To be eliminated[cxli]. But the relationship between soil and capital constitutes co-action[cxlii] and natural conflict. Neither[cxliii] can be denied (R.Beelevf). Co-action where soil is subject to alternative demands has reached an expanse[cxliv] into spaces of non-difference at a specific moment (R.Beelevf). Fragments, united, are arranged in a way[cxlv] that is specific to capital. The commodity chain[cxlvi] serves capital. Capital is linear[cxlvii]. Capital as logic is fertilizer[cxlviii] as commodity. Fertilizer is an agent[cxlix] of production: a cotton farmer buys fertilizer. The fertilizer is given a price[cl]. The fertilizer is in the hands[cli] of a cotton farmer. The fertilizer is not in the hands of the farmer for very long[clii]. The speed of capital is integrated[cliii] into the natural cycles of planting and harvesting cotton. The soil and the cotton farmer are enclosed by the city$_{cliv}$. The home has a social and spatial relationship with the soil$_{clv}$. The home$_{clvi}$ is the site of production for the cotton farmer and the farmer's community. The accumulation of profit flows away$_{clvii}$ from the site and the means of production. This oppositional flow erodes social space and destroys the fabric of those who own$_{clviii}$ the means of production. The flow of money from cotton travels$_{clix}$ away from the farmer's home. Some farmers need to follow the logic$_{clx}$ of capital. Money$_{clxi}$ flows elsewhere, and this is logic. The same logic$_{clxii}$ as fertilizer. Death$_{clxiii}$. With fertilizer$_{clxiv}$, the farmer has a choice. To reproduce the means$_{clxv}$ of production. To reproduce$_{clxvi}$ capital. To reproduce the structure where profit from soil and cotton flow out of the home$_{clxvii}$, away from socially necessary labor. Watch$_{clxviii}$ the topsoil erode. Or enter$_{clxix}$ the ruptured surface. The choice$_{clxx}$ is inescapable. There is a moment when the farmer changes the dominant narrative to work[clxxi] from a space of autonomy. Farmers in India die of suicide[clxxii] by drinking their own fertilizer.* The hidden transcript is led by the farmer's relationship with the soil[clxxiii]. The farmer changes the land and its social relations[clxxiv] by choosing not to reproduce its conditions. Not to re-enact[clxxv]. To act[clxxvi]. To be a *persona*[clxxvii]. The *persona* must perform because the ecology[clxxviii] is inescapable. Body[clxxix] and space are inescapable. Real *persona* reveals[clxxx] human nature. This is the site of intervention[clxxxi]. But whom[clxxxii] or what will the *persona* serve (V.E.Swenjiakh)? Performance[clxxxiii]. Death[clxxxiv]. To reconnect[clxxxv] the farmer with the soil. Land[clxxxvi] with labor. Nothing[clxxxvii] disappears completely (R.Beelevf). Site-specificity[clxxxviii]. Rupture[clxxxix]. How far to distance from the point[cxc] of rupture? How

* In fact, these farmers usually consume pesticides. Pesticides and fertilizers are, in reality, strictly connected in their process of soil depletion.

far$_{cxci}$ will one go to live close to it, or far from it?

Fertilizer reflects$_{cxcii}$ the application and practice of local knowledge. But where does this knowledge$_{cxciii}$ come from? What does it remove$_{cxciv}$? Work$_{cxcv}$ in relation to soil. The soil is sanitized$_{cxcvi}$. To remove dirt$_{cxcvii}$. To sanitize the water around the soil$_{cxcviii}$. Soil erosion$_{cxcix}$. Topsoil sanitizes the nearest$_{cc}$ fields. It rarely touches$_{cci}$ cement, unless a different environmental disaster happens because of sanitized soil. It sanitizes the home$_{ccii}$. The home as the site of production is also the closest$_{cciii}$ thing to soil that is worked by the cotton farmer. The farmer's hands touch$_{cciv}$ the soil. Fertilizer touches the hands$_{ccv}$ of the farmer. The home is exposed$_{ccvi}$ to fertilizer. The clothes$_{ccvii}$ that the farmer wears when working the soil enters the home. Where it touches$_{ccviii}$ whatever and whoever is closest. This home$_{ccix}$ is somehow unquarantined.

This situation is very different from other sectors on the factory floor[ccx] of the garment manufacturing industry. The zoning of the garment manufacturing industry in New York City represents a different[ccxi] kind of protection and sanitation. Sanitize the soil[ccxii]. Sanitize the farmer[ccxiii]. Sanitize the home[ccxxiv]. Sanitize the community[ccxxv]. The fertilizer is felt by those closest to the raw[ccxxvi] source. Fertilizer[ccxxvii] is not soil. Nothing[ccxxviii] disappears completely (R.Beelevf). Knowledge perceives a logic that places demands[ccxxix] on soil and cotton. The relationship between[ccxxx] the farmer and the soil is defined by an intrinsic knowledge. The farmer knows the soil needs to be treated[ccxxxi] right and cannot be abused (S.Biens). The cotton farmer knows the soil by touch, smell, every input to its composition, and the conditions that change the soil's property[ccxxxii]. These thought processes are conceived and created, even if the farmer is enclosed[ccxxxiii].

Built[ccxxxiv] in mind. The process may be held until the remembrance finds a space in which to break the surface[ccxxxv] and perform. But scientific thought says to manipulate[ccxxxvi] the soil. The contradiction[ccxxxvii] is the site specificity. The space[ccxxxviii] rises from productive action (R.Beelevf). Absolute enclosure[ccxxxix] over site-specificity. We should sensitize ourselves to the location[ccxl]. To do what needs to be done and to understand what needs to be understood[ccxli] (Y.Evrah). The entire dirty[ccxlii] process. If not, the entire process is sanitized and killed of all difference[ccxliii]. Which has already happened to the profit and transformation[ccxliv] of soil and cotton [fertilizer], [farmer] (R.Beelevf). This newly incorporated, sanitized, and institutionalized space used to be the farthest from this saleable representation[ccxlv] (R.Beelevf). The concept that is easiest to understand is the binary[ccxlvi] narrative (R.Beelevf).

Easy because it is sanitized[ccxlvii] (R.Beelevf). It is easy to follow a progressive line that leads to an enclosure without considering its relationship with the source[ccxlviii] (R.Beelevf): soil[ccxlix]. The precise, site-specific enclosure becomes shattered[ccl]. Orderly[ccli] collusion. A place[cclii] less easy to navigate. But this is the exact time and place to act[ccliii]. Because it is the source of the escape[ccliv]. Yet inescapable[cclv] no matter where one looks.

The owner of the source[cclvi] is within the owner of the surplus of the resource. The genesis[cclvii] and tracing of its provenance lead to death as product (R.Beelevf). Soil now has no limits[cclviii] to entry (R.Beelevf). The space of contradiction is not questioned[cclix] (R.Beelevf). Mechanisms that constitute the mechanism ensure operability[cclx] (R.Beelevf). Soil is not an empty box to be filled[cclxi] (R.Beelevf). Soil does not lack agency[cclxii], intelligence

(R.Beelevf). Soil cannot be uprooted and displaced into a constructed[cclxiii] whole (R.Beelevf). The urban land[cclxiv] in New York City needs an injection of value. The garment manufacturing[cclxv] zone is displaced from the source (R.Beelevf). It assumes that nature requires displacement in order to function[cclxvi] as a system (R.Beelevf). Capital validates a system to fragments of soil, rendering both soil and cotton as lifeless and powerless[cclxvii] (R.Beelevf). The relatively infinite becomes absolutely finite[cclxviii] (R.Beelevf). Scarcity and death are repeated, elaborated, and consumed for a final commodity as package[cclxix] (R.Beelevf). There is no sector between what we know and hold[cclxx] in our hands (R.Beelevf). Absolute authority is deep-rooted[cclxxi] (R.Beelevf). It holds soil together with farmers and a value-added industry along its chain[cclxxii]. Held together, despite separate[cclxxiii] from the source (R.Beelevf). Held together to elaborate and to reproduce jointed and disjointed chains as isolated property[cclxxiv] (R.Beelevf). All of this originates[cclxxv] from production. State capitalist regulations and mechanisms of industry kill soil and labor[cclxxvi] (R.Beelevf). A single act initiated by a single farmer in a single space spiral[cclxxvii] outward. Urban use has extended over the land to the point where it is less augmented by adoration and offering to its fertility[cclxxviii] (R.Beelevf + Y.Evrah). Would powers[cclxxix] in the city's garment industry risk destroying their own source (R.Beelevf)? Fixed tools of the absolute presuppose the soil and the farmer to be physical remains[cclxxx] and nothing more (R.Beelevf). The mechanisms[cclxxxi] of power dominate over matter and soil to destroy it and all of its surroundings (R.Beelevf). The soil is agitated[cclxxxii] (R.Beelevf). The soil is institutionalized[cclxxxiii]. Uprooted[cclxxxiv]. So is the ecology of soil[cclxxxv]. The corpses of nature are marketed as a package[cclxxxvi] in a built box, in the boxes that envelope our society (R.Beelevf). Soil is exchangeable because it is scarce[cclxxxvii] (R.Beelevf). Soil is pushed into a reproductive[cclxxxviii] cycle that it does not own (R.Beelevf). Soil's only value[cclxxxix] is to be an exchangeable thing (R.Beelevf). Soil has no worth when[ccxc] farmers are attached to the land by an exchangeable value rather than a socially necessary labor process (R.Beelevf). The methodical reduction of soil treats it as a disciplining doctrine[ccxci] (R.Beelevf). This seeks the extraction[ccxcii] of data from soil rather than recognizes its political agency in relation to the economy and labor (R.Beelevf). Soil relocates[ccxciii] to a silo. The soil and the farmer lose their use value[ccxciv]. The soil and the farmer are made into a new, exclusive[ccxcv] economic transaction. They are injected with the same value as a silo[ccxcvi] that is used for storage. Some people cut throats with a knife[ccxcvii]. Some[ccxcviii] with cotton.

[4] My production process[i] operates as a representation of space. It is explained in this specific footnote, a process footnote[ii], which is identified as number 4. This text is void of visuals because it acts as a drawing[iii] to be read. In ACT ONE, footnote number 4 appears[iv] directly after the period at the end of a single sentence. That one, single sentence is composed of four[v] single boxes. These four boxes are linked together[vi] by the spaces [in between] each box with plus signs. Each single box then forms[vii] one entire sequence. It is a commodity chain that functions as a representation of space, an image[viii] of one unit from within the whole. Footnote number 4 represents a place of operation[ix]. It is outside[x] the entire composition of four linked boxes that form one entire sentence, one entire sequence, one entire production chain of one commodity: cotton. Footnote number[xi] 1 is a symbol. It is a placeholder for the word[xii] cotton. Cotton is a single

number, a single unit enveloped[xiii] within the space of one sentence. Here, the sequence represents one box as one commodity as package, and one value from one raw[xiv] material: cotton. Both originating from and represented by footnote number 1, cotton[1] expresses a value that is reduced[xv] and defined as a proportion so that the entire sentence functions as a chain. However, the sentence is more[xvi] complex than its representation. It is composed of more than a single cotton material[xvii]. The entire sentence has four individual units that must be broken[xviii] down in order to understand its entire structure. Four boxes are linked[xix] within one whole unit: 4 = 1. This one sentence produces not only the space of a commodity chain as sentence but also one layer[xx] of complexity: topsoil[xxi]. It is one moment in time, ACT ONE, fixed in a particular place with a particular purpose[xxii]: a cotton[1] farmer[2] buys fertilizer[3]. This sentence portrays[xxiii] one layer of topsoil. Topsoil is the surface layer that is located above[xxiv] the complex structure of soil. Soil is beneath[xxv] this layer of topsoil. The soil is hidden[xxvi]. Soil is the source[xxvii] of the sentence. Soil is the source of cotton[xxviii]. Soil is the source of the commodity chain[xxix]. Soil is the source that transforms the cottonseed[xxx] into a final packaged good. One single garment[xxxi] originating from one single chain is composed of a reduction of a thing combined with other things, where the things themselves appear to have nothing to do with each other. But through this process of production plus reduction, abstraction[xxxii] individuates cotton within an absolute whole. Topsoil simulates[xxxiii] soil. So the sentence as commodity chain requires a breaking down of its sequence in order to understand its complexity[xxxiv]. By letting both the sentence and the commodity chain come apart, we find these four units, which must be broken down even further[xxxv].

We find not only a linear[xxxvi] commodity chain but also a horizontal layer of topsoil. One single commodity chain, one single unit of the commodity chain[xxxvii]. This one single layer[xxxviii] of topsoil needs to fall apart. The eyes[xxxix] are passive but labor is active (R.Beelevf).

Footnote number 2[xl]: farmer[2]. Farmer is represented by the value[xli] of 2, that is, one single value represented as a unit. Abstraction[xlii], reduction. An image of space functions as a fragment[xliii] based on its role in the sentence. The farmer has a function[xliv] in the commodity chain and a relationship with what surrounds the individual unit. Farmer, symbolized[xlv] by the value of 2, implies the farmer's relation to the farmer's location within the soil's surface. Footnote number 1, cotton[1], plus footnote number 2, farmer[2], appear[xlvi] to be different, separate — without touching or relating. But there is an empty[xlvii], unseen space in between footnotes 1 and 2. The relationship of differences[xlviii] within a structure appear to be one in the same. The complexity produced by the space between footnotes 1 and 2, as reproductions[xlix] of a larger space, is not all we see. To understand footnote number 1, we must also break down footnote number 2 to grasp both 1 and 2 as individual values and how 1 + 2 relate based on the space that is produced[l]. These represented values[li] are produced for us to see. We see numbers[lii] 1 and 2. We also see the logical link[liii] as a plus sign, but there is still a space in between 1 + 2 that we do not see. Even though we do not see this space, or a relation to it, this does not mean that a space does not exist between[liv] cotton[1] and farmer[2], between 1 and 2, or 1 + 2. We see[lv] only what has been produced for us to see. To consume[lvi]. The eyes are passive[lvii] but labor is active (R.Beelevf): A cotton[1] farmer[2] buys.

To buy[lviii] is an act that is performed at a specific time and in a specific place to serve a particular purpose.

Footnote number 3 represents fertilizer[lix]. Fertilizer is a value that is added to the soil to increase its productive capacity, which cotton farmers then consume into their own bodies to escape[lx] their debt-ridden land. Fertilizer increases[lxi] cotton production. Fertilizer decreases[lxii] the number of farmers needed to produce cotton. Fertilizer is a commodity[lxiii]. Fertilizer, represented by the value of 3, also needs to be broken down in order to understand its individual properties[lxiv], how they relate to each other, and how they relate to the other values in the sentence's composition. Fertilizer, value 3, relates[lxv] to value 2: farmer[2], identified as value[lxvi] 2, is to the left of fertilizer[3]. Values 2 and 3 are mediated[lxvii] by an act, a purpose in a place and at a moment in time: a turning[lxviii] point based on price.

Supply$_{\mathrm{lxix}}$. Demand$_{\mathrm{lxx}}$. Who or what is subject$_{\mathrm{lxxi}}$ to the demands produced by this space of exchange. A market place for buying and selling, where uses are reduced to exchangeable properties, dictated$_{\mathrm{lxxii}}$ by a form that facilitates and maintains the exchange of goods, and the relations surrounding their exchange. Nothing$_{\mathrm{lxxiii}}$ disappears completely (R.Beelevf). As a commodity, like the farmer$_{\mathrm{lxxiv}}$, the farmer's production of work. Plus the farmer's time consumed$_{\mathrm{lxxv}}$ for the production of such work as a commodity. Cotton$_{\mathrm{lxxvi}}$. Fertilizer is also a commodity, one with a particular agency$_{\mathrm{lxxvii}}$. Fertilizer, represented by value 3$_{\mathrm{lxxviii}}$, functions as an agent that is in relation to and alongside. In the sentence, it is situated$_{\mathrm{lxxix}}$ after the word *buys* between farmer[2] and fertilizer[3]. Buys is a sign$_{\mathrm{lxxx}}$ that brings the word farmer to fertilizer: farmer[2] buys fertilizer[3]. This phrase is placed$_{\mathrm{lxxxi}}$ directly after cotton[1] and is entirely in topsoil. The sentence's full$_{\mathrm{lxxxii}}$

composition is situated in topsoil. Fertilizer possesses an agency that has the productive capacity to change the composition[lxxxiii] of not only the sentence but also the topsoil structure. This happens through a process of topsoil decomposition[lxxxiv]. But fertilizer also possesses an agency that has the productive capacity to change[lxxxv] the composition of the farmer through a value-added sign and yet another process of decomposition. The fertilizer possesses the productive capacity for the farmer to be decomposed by the soil[lxxxvi]. Indeed, this relationship is facilitated by the word[lxxxvii] *buys*. An act[lxxxviii]. A moment[lxxxix]. A purchase[xc], facilitated by capital. Despite distance, capital can transform relations from above and below by arranging reductions[xci] into a value that is exchangeable across time and space. The composition of spatial[xcii] relations is transformed. The sentence's composition is situated within[xciii] a layer of topsoil for three reasons: cotton[1], farmer[2], and fertilizer[3]. The structure of this sentence addresses a perceived challenge with theory and representation[xciv]. The words cotton[1], farmer[2], and fertilizer[3] are actors[xcv] within the entire structure, working in relation to each other. Their actions reproduce[xcvi] the sentence structure, or not. Each action depends[xcvii] on whom or what the *persona* serves. All individual parts can be rearranged[xcviii] to serve the particular ways in which the structure of the whole composition functions. The space in between each of the four parts[xcix] acts as an opening, a rupture within a space that has not been produced. We gaze[c] toward what is produced. The sentence structure shows us words in a sentence that follow[ci] a line and a specific logic. The composition and the process[cii] dictates the sequence.

Footnote number 4 defines[ciii] the internal process from the outside. The space in between, the relationships, are the breaks in the sentence, the openings, the frailties[civ] of the entire system of the sentence. If detected from within the system, this frailty can break the chain to reconfigure[cv] it based on the relations seen from the inside out. Still, what remains within the sentence needs to be broken down[cvi] further.

The production process[cvii] of cotton is complex, and how to represent this complexity is a challenge. A solution would be to narrow the content[cviii] of this text into one single unit like cotton or soil. But to engage with a process of narrowing a focus would be to mimic the representation of the single[cix] structure from which we operate. To narrow the focus of this text to just cotton would deny[cx] other processes that exist in relation to cotton. This would blind[cxi] the processes used to uncover these relations. A single structure denies the complexity and therefore denies the reality of our lives through a process of sanitization[cxii]. This is done by reproducing a single framework viewed from a single, narrow[cxiii] lens that reproduces our labor process. However, processes of labor and processes that relate to labor possess multiple, varying breaks on the surface[cxiv]. Topsoil is the surface layer[cxv] of soil. Topsoil can be dowsed[cxvi] with a dowser. An opening in the surface layer breaks up the topsoil, where a broken surface layer can be picked up and placed together — even if the relationships are perceived as illogical (simply because it has never been seen or no one has pointed us where[cxvii] to look). For a moment[cxviii], we may be able to understand something that has been present all the time, shifting all the way, alongside. An understanding[cxix] that comes from a complex structure, for a moment, is not reproduced. From one opening, we are led to see beneath[cxx] the topsoil. Deeper into[cxxi] the layers of soil. Soil[cxxii] is the source of the entire sentence. However, soil does not appear[cxxiii] in the sentence structure of the topsoil layer: [A cotton[1] farmer[2] buys fertilizer[3].[4]]. The source[cxxiv], [soil], is hidden. The source is removed from the sentence and buried[cxxv]. Instead of placing a narrow focus on one concept in a single sentence, the sentence is undone[cxxvi]. Situated in soil, one can initiate[cxxvii] a process of understanding complex systems by undoing the words that serve the sentence structure. [cotton[1]] is the starting point[cxxviii] of the commodity chain. Cotton represents capital[cxxix], which maintains the entire commodity chain of the sentence. [farmer[2]] represents labor, specifically labor in relation[cxxx] to cotton[1]. [fertilizer[3]] represents land[cxxxi].

Within these words of cotton[1], farmer[2], fertilizer[3], and process[4], multiple, variant intricacies are interpreted through a system of footnotes that operate$_{cxxxii}$ as layers within a complex soil structure beneath the primary surface layer of topsoil. Each individual footnote of 1, 2, 3, and 4 is reproduced$_{cxxxiii}$. The elaboration of each footnote is held together by a system$_{cxxxiv}$ of Roman numerals that begins with the value "i". Each Roman numeral is attached to one specific word in a sentence, where the same Roman numeral is then mirrored$_{cxxxv}$, reproduced, and extended to the next sentence, leading a direct, linear progression from point [i] in one sentence to point [ii] in the next sentence. See, for example, the following progression$_{cxxxvi}$ of numbers within this Roman numeral system that never starts with zero: [^{1} Cotton$_i$ is a commodity. Cotton comes from a seed$_{ii}$. A cottonseed is placed into the ground by a farmer$_{iii}$.]. Each sentence continues$_{cxxxvii}$ to thread, depending on the production of the previous sentence. This leads us deeper$_{cxxxviii}$ into the soil until the word [soil] is found, written for the first time. There are many complex layers[cxxxix] of soil beneath the topsoil, so when reaching [soil] for the first time, as a hidden source within the topsoil sentence structure, the reader should stop and take notice before going deeper. The deeper we go, the more complex the situation, so we must: 1. start from a representation; 2. find what is [hidden], and 3. represent, in a new way, what is found[cxl]. The word[cxli] *soil* does not appear until we read the fertilizer[3] footnote. Here[cxlii], fertilizer[3] represents land. Nothing[cxliii] disappears completely (R.Beelevf).

There is also a coding system for each source[cxliv] used throughout the text. The sources exist like soil[cxlv] as a source: hidden[cxlvi]. I wrote each source as one single sentence on a notecard, then attached[cxlvii] a sticky note with my own translation of each concept. In nearly every case, not a single word was transferred directly[cxlviii] from the source. I then categorized[cxlix] and organized each notecard with my sticky note into a cotton[1] pile, a farmer[2] pile, a fertilizer[3] pile, or a process[4] pile. There was a lot to compost[cl]. Once each notecard was placed into one of these four categories, I then organized each category into a linear[cli] progression of sourced notecards as a placeholder within the sequence of my text, represented as an order of operations. I then created[clii] a second coding system to represent the citation of sources. I took the last name from each author[cliii] and removed one letter from each last name (or two letters, depending on the last name and/or number of authors from one specific source). The letter that I excised[cliv] from the source's last name then served as the initial of the first letter of a pseudonym so that the author could not be identified in the text. After this reduction process of removing one letter from each last name as a proportion lesser than the whole, I rearranged the remaining[clv] letters of each author's last name into a new last name, see, for example: R.Max = Karl Marx. Each newly constructed last name, plus its first initial, serves as a hidden source that repeats and disperses unevenly[clvi] throughout the soil complex. Nothing disappears[clvii] completely (R.Beelevf). Each source is based on my own interpretation[clviii], except for two sentences. The first[clix] is: "Nothing disappears completely." This citation comes directly from The Production of Space by Henri Lefebvre, Chapter 4 "From Absolute Space to Abstract Space" (as it appears in the second sentence in Section I, Page 229 in the 1991 edition[clx] from Blackwell Publishing, based on the 1974 original). However, in my text, this specific sentence from Lefebvre, repeated throughout my text, is not represented as a fragment of its original[clxi]. The entire sentence that appears[clxii] in Lefebvre's The Production of Space reads as follows:

"Nothing disappears completely, however; nor can what subsists be defined solely in terms of traces, memories or relics." Regarding my specific text, the representation of three words are sufficient to serve the function of the text as a whole[clxiii], see: Nothing disappears completely (R.Beelevf). The second, and final, direct quote used once in my text[clxiv] is by Hans Haacke: "A better word than honour is human dignity. The latter tends to keep the individual in mind." (from Hans Haacke, Phaidon Press Limited, London 1994, as it appears on Page 97). This remains as a direct quotation because my own words seemed[clxv] insufficient for translation. It is also important to note that there may be errors in the implementation, reproduction, and elaboration of the Roman numeral system[clxvi] within the text. The sequence[clxvii] should be as precise as possible. However, since the sequencing process was as sanitized[clxviii] as much as possible, and with any system breakdown, the surface area of my working environment was not as sterile as it appears. Meaning, following the Roman numeral system, errors may materialize beneath the topsoil, making the surface less than spotless[clxix]. Then again, we look[clxx] where we are told to look.

A third and final source (but first and only appearance[clxxi]) in direct quotation form is as follows: "The passive body (the senses) and the active body (labour) converge in space." from The Production of Space by Henri Lefebvre. The composition of any sentence is not as clear[clxxii] as it looks. And by situating myself in soil, I found[clxxiii] that nothing disappears completely.

WORKS SOURCED
IN ORDER OF APPEARANCE

R.BEELEVF[LEFEBVRE]
[LEFEBVRE]Henri
[The Production of Space]

F.Z.FERIGEWINKEIZCO[GEREFFI + KORZENIEWICZ]
[GEREFFI]Gary + [KORZENIEWICZ]Miguel
[Commodity Chains and Global Capitalism]

Y.EVRAH[HARVEY]
[HARVEY]David
[Social Justice and the City]

A.CHEAK[HAACKE]
[HAACKE]Hans
[Hans Haacke]

I.CHATPAR[PACHIRAT]
[PACHIRAT]Timothy
[Every Twelve Seconds: Industrialized
Slaughter and the Politics of Sight]

R.MAX[MARX]
[MARX]Karl
[Capital vol. 3]

L.NEUGE[LE GUIN]
[LE GUIN]Ursula
[The Dispossessed]

G.N.N.P.HVAINDBVAMDIORO^{GANDHI + NAMBOODIRI}
^{GANDHI}Vasant P. + ^{NAMBOODIRI}N.V.
[The Adoption and Economics
of Bt Cotton in India]

C.TOTS^{SCOTT}
^{SCOTT}James C.
[Domination and the Arts of Resistance:
Hidden Transcripts]

Ć.MAROVAIB^{ABRAMOVIĆ}
^{ABRAMOVIĆ}Marina
[The Artist is Present]

V.E.SWENJIAKH^{van HEESWIJK}
^{van HEESWIJK}Jeanne
[The Artist Will Have to Decide
Whom to Serve]

S.BIENS^{BISSEN}
^{BISSEN}Tom
[Conversation on Soil, May 2013]

9 788889 405056 1